IMAGES OF CANADA

IMAGES

OF

CANADA

Text by Phil Surguy

From
Judy and Brian
Xmas 1983.

Discovery Books

The heart of this book is the popular "Images of Canada" series of photographs which ran in **Today Magazine,** a weekend supplement that appeared in eighteen newspapers across the country. The series began in January 1982 and continued until August 28 of that year, when **Today Magazine** ceased publication.

Canadian Cataloguing in Publication Data
Main entry under title:
Images of Canada

Includes index.
ISBN 0-919493-08-4

1. Canada—Description and travel—1950—Views

FC59.I42 917.1'04646'0222 C83-094003-0
F1016.I42

Produced by Discovery Books for:
Classic Bookshops,
98 Carrier Drive,
Rexdale, Ontario. M9W 5R1

Designed by Patrick Chung, Graphic Atelier, Canada.

Printed and bound in Hong Kong.

FRONT COVER: Waterton Lakes National Park, on the U.S. border in southwestern Alberta. It is the Canadian half of the Waterton-Glacier International Peace Park.

BACK COVER: Downtown, St. John's, Newfoundland. Hunting near Truro, Nova Scotia. Thunderclouds gathering over an Alberta grain field.

PAGE 1: Skating on Lost Lagoon, at the entrance to Stanley Park, Vancouver, British Columbia. The local climate is so mild that the lagoon accumulates ice thick enough for skating only once every four years, and the ice never lasts more than two weeks.

PAGE 2: The town of Trinity, Trinity Bay, Newfoundland, one of the first European settlements in North America.

RIGHT: The Church of the Immaculate Conception, Cooks Creek, Manitoba. Called the "Prairie Cathedral", it was built in the second quarter of this century by the people of the Ukrainian Catholic farming community it serves.

Contents

A late summer field hockey game in High Park, Toronto, Ontario.

Introduction

Even the North Pole is a tourist attraction these days. It wasn't so very long ago that Canada was seen by Europeans as little more than a vast snowbound, scarcely habitable *terra incognita* blocking their way to the riches of China and India. Sir Martin Frobisher, John Davis, Henry Hudson, William Baffin and Sir John Franklin were only a few of the navigators who tried to sail around Canada, searching for a way to the Orient through the ice-clogged Arctic islands. Hudson's expedition claimed his life in 1611. Franklin and his crew disappeared in 1847. Actual navigation of the Northwest Passage was not achieved until Roald Amundsen's voyage of 1903-1906, and by then the air age had begun.

Today, if you have $7,000 and ten days to spare, you can fly from Edmonton to the North Pole. It's a three-stage journey over territory that many of those early explorers starved or froze to death without ever seeing. First you fly to Resolute Bay on Cornwallis Island, then to Lake Hazen on Ellesmere Island (about as far north as you can go and still be in Canada) and from there, via skiplane, to the Pole, where you stand around being exhilarated by the wonder of it all while sipping champagne and munching cavier on toast. On the return flight, weather permitting, the plane touches down at the North Magnetic Pole and you are served a beer and a sausage roll. Back in Resolute Bay, according to the tour operator's brochure, you can "take a snowmobile trip on the historic Northwest Passage.... Then, prior to boarding PWA's Flight 582 to Edmonton, enjoy a farewell drink at Canada's most northerly bar, the Resolute Airport Arctic Club."

That's Canada. In the last 350-odd years the land has provided to be rich, eminently habitable and not quite so snowbound as the first European visitors thought. Today, at work and at play, Canadians easily traverse their country in all manner of aircraft, boat and vehicle, including one-seater microlight planes, rubber rafts, dune buggies and giant earth-moving machines that are custom-built for the herculean jobs they do. Much of the final exploration of the country is being accomplished by satellite and airplane.

Despite the fact that there is now virtually nowhere in Canada that we can't go to and live year-round if we have the mind to, few Canadians feel that the land has been conquered or even tamed. The Canadian landscape is too big, too diverse, too downright potent for its small population to have yet done much more than come to terms with it, and perhaps only temporarily at that. For not all of Canada is 350-odd years old. Vancouver, the country's third largest city, was not incorporated until 1886. The town of Faro, in the Yukon, was built in 1969, and new towns and cities are still being dreamed of and planned. In other words, Canada is still a long way from being a settled country in the sense that, say, France is.

Canada covers an area of 3,851,787 square miles. At its broadest, the country is more than 3,000 miles wide; and the Trans-Canada Highway, the main east-west route, which connects the cities and towns of southern Canada where most of the nation's 24 million people live, is 4,900 miles long. From the northern tip of Ellesmere Island to the southernmost place in Canada—Pelee Island, located in Lake Erie—the distance is about 2,800 miles.

Almost 10 percent of Canada's area is made up of lakes and rivers. The hydroelectric potential of these waters has only begun to be tapped, and there are dreamers and schemers who spend a lot of their time thinking about how they might divert Canada's fresh water reserves to thirsty regions of the United States and Mexico. But perhaps the greatest significance of Canada's lakes and rivers is their continuing importance as natural passageways through a vast, often difficult and sometimes impassable landscape. For instance, the St. Lawrence-Great Lakes system (a 2,500-mile route from the Gulf of St. Lawrence to Thunder Bay on the western shore of Lake Superior) has been the primary avenue to the interior of Canada from the very beginning of European exploration. Today the waterway, with the roads and railways that have been built beside it, is more important than ever as a carrier of raw materials and finished goods, and the country's two largest cities, Toronto and Montreal,

A small-town rodeo in southwestern Saskatchewan. There are still many working cowboys in western Canada, and local rodeos are an important part of their social life.

as well as many other major processing and manufacturing centres are located along it.

French fur traders were the first Europeans to use the St. Lawrence-Great Lakes system. From settlements in the St. Lawrence Valley, they steadily made their way west until, in the early 18th century, they were trading with Indians in the heart of the continent. This brought them into conflict with the British, who were trading out of posts they had established on Hudson Bay. Both British and French traders dreamed of and searched for a northwest passage to the Pacific, but furs were their main business, and the two sides were virtually at war for more than 100 years.

In 1713, when France relinquished to Britain its claim to the territory draining into Hudson Bay (which included most of the Prairies), the Montreal-based traders continued to fight the British-owned Hudson's Bay Company for control of the area. The British took Quebec in 1759, but the battle for the fur trade still went on—until 1821, when the Montreal traders merged their business with the Hudson's Bay Company. The union gave the company absolute control over all of what is now continental Canada lying north and west of the St. Lawrence-Great Lakes region— right out to the Pacific Ocean and up to the Arctic shores. Few countries—*few empires*— have been as large as the Hudson's Bay Company's domain, but little encouragement was given to immigration and development of the territory. It was a private trading preserve.

Initially, the most substantial European settlement in Canada was French. French settlers followed the fur traders to the St. Lawrence Valley and founded Quebec. And on the Atlantic coast the prosperous French colony of Acadia occupied most of the area that now comprises the provinces of Nova Scotia, New Brunswick and Prince Edward Island. France ceded Acadia to Britain in 1713. The British captured Quebec 46 years later, and for about two decades after that the future provinces of Atlantic Canada were simply the northernmost of Britain's American colonies.

Then came the American Revolution and the War of 1812, two very important events in Canadian history. Thousands of Americans who remained loyal to Britain fled north. Most went to Nova Scotia and New Brunswick, but a large number took refuge in western Quebec, which had two far-reaching results. First, the Quebecois were effectively surrounded by English-speaking people. And second, the land the western Loyalists settled, was severed from Quebec and became the foundation of modern Ontario. At first, though, it was called Upper Canada. Quebec was known for a time as Lower Canada.

Despite, or because of, the example to the south, the idea of creating a Canadian nation did not take hold until well into the 19th century. The first official step toward nationhood was taken in 1864, when representatives from Upper and Lower Canada went to Charlottetown, Prince Edward Island, to attend a conference at which delegates from Nova Scotia, New Brunswick and Prince Edward Island were discussing union of the Maritime provinces. The self-governing Dominion of Canada was created by an act of the British Parliament three years later.

The four original members of the new dominion were Upper Canada, Lower Canada, New Brunswick and Nova Scotia. Prince Edward Island joined in 1873. The enormous domain of the Hudson's Bay Company was bought by Canada in 1869 and over the years the four western provinces were created: Manitoba in 1870; British Columbia in 1871; and Alberta and Saskatchewan in 1905. The colony of Newfoundland did not become a province until 1949. Joey Smallwood, the driving force behind Newfoundland's move, is still alive, which means that, more than a century after Confederation began, Canada has a living father of the country.

Creating a geographical and administrative entity called Canada is one thing. However, creating a settled, developed and truly unified nation is an entirely different process—one that has continued since 1867 with new quirks and wrinkles arising every generation, and may continue for another century.

The transcontinental railways, completed at the end of the 19th century, provided the country's fundamental unifying links (and, incidentally, realized the dream of a viable northwest passage, enabling goods from the Orient to be rushed across the continent, notably on the elite, highballing silk trains which had the right of way all across the country). But the railroads changed Canada in another dramatic way: between 1890 and 1914, they brought an estimated three million central European immigrants to the farmlands of the Prairies. Before that, immigrants to Canada had largely been people from the British Isles, who generally settled in the older parts of the country. Now, the British majority is steadily being eroded, and almost all Canadian cities have large, dynamic populations that have, since the Second World War, come to Canada from everywhere in Asia, Europe and the West Indies. The population of Toronto includes one of the largest Italian-speaking communities in the world.

Canada has grown into a big, awkward, precocious adolescent of a nation. At one extreme, Canadians are working at the forefront of the new satellite, video and biological technologies. At another extreme, the people of the north, mainly Indians and Eskimos (who prefer to be called Dene and Inuit) still make a large part of their living by hunting and trapping. As much as 85 percent of the country remains wild and uninhabited. In the Northwest Territories, huge herds of migratory caribou, at times 100,000 strong, still roam freely. In the dense bush not far from Vancouver there is persistent, often persuasive evidence of the existence of a giant, shy, ape-like creature called the sasquatch. The country's climate and vegetation range from the profuse rain forest of the Pacific coast to the delicate flowers that proliferate during the brief Arctic growing season.

After Confederation, Canada's economic and political power became concentrated in Ontario. In recent years, however, there has been a massive emigration to the west, and there are people who believe that the country's economic power (largely as a result of Alberta's oil boom) is shifting in that direction, too. Moreover, the other regions have become stronger, more self-confident and assertive. Quebec recently elected its most nationalistic government ever. Newfoundland and Nova Scotia are flexing their muscles in anticipation of the offshore oil developments that might turn their region into another Alberta. And even the 60,000 people who inhabit the northern third of the country have begun to demand the right to determine how their territories are governed and developed.

Canada is a nation of perpetual change. Some people believe that the generally low-key Canadian personality is a product of an oppressive climate. That's not true. All regions of the country have gorgeous summers of varying duration, and Canadians have learned to play with the winter, engaging in all manner of outdoor activities, from hockey to cross-country skiing. Many Canadians happily sit outside in the winter to watch professional football games. No, the weather is not the reason why Canadians, to the bemusement of foreigners, rarely get hysterical about social and political concerns. The reason is that Canadian history has been one of almost incessant change, which has for the most part worked out quite well without everyone becoming too excited; and the future, Canadians know, promises to be more of the same, as Canada proceeds with the long task of defining itself as a nation.

Street artists are one of the hundreds of attractions in old, walled Quebec City, Quebec.

OVERLEAF: A rape seed crop near Innisfree, east of Edmonton, Alberta.

In a manner akin to the condescending way
that New Yorkers regard California, many
Eastern Canadians like to think of British
Columbia as a Lotusland populated by self-
absorbed kooks who have been laid back to
the point of torpor by the easy life that is there
for the asking. Actually, very few people get a
free ride in British Columbia, and the California analogy is apt in only two narrow senses.
First, the climate, particularly in the southwestern coastal region, is the best in the country.
And second, people in the far west have the
resources and space to realize their potential
in individual and dramatic ways, free of the
colonial and European attitudes that govern
so much of life in the east. This was true even
of the Haida, Kwakiutl and other coastal
peoples. Taking full advantage of the climate
and the wealth offered by the forests and the
sea, they evolved the most spectacular art and
culture north of the Aztec civilization. West
Coast Indian art was only beginning to reach
its peak when Cook, Vancouver and other
British navigators arrived at the end of the
18th century.

Victoria, British Columbia's beautiful capital, began as a trading post in 1843. It was
named the capital of the crown colony of
Vancouver Island in 1852 and became a
booming port and supply centre in 1858,
when the first British Columbia gold rushes
started. Today British Columbia occupies
366,255 square miles, most of them mountain-
ous. Agriculture is largely confined to the
Fraser River delta, the Peace River country,
the Texas-sized ranches of the interior plateau
and the orchards of the Okanagan Valley. The
bulk of the province's wealth—in timber, pulp,
paper, minerals and hydroelectric power —
comes from the mountains. Thus, the majority
of the population lives in valleys or on the
sides of mountains, and the natural impulse
of people in such circumstances is to find out
what's in the next valley, and the one after that.

That is what British Columbians do. The
province isn't there just to be worked. It's to
be explored and enjoyed as well. And at every
opportunity British Columbians get out, to
engage in every conceivable type of outdoor
recreation, or simply to tour, marveling at the
infinite beauty and variety, with an increasing
sense that the entire province is their own.

British Columbia

Mount Garibaldi Provincial Park, a short drive north of Vancouver, British Columbia.

RIGHT: The Rocky Mountains of British Columbia. In many centres in British Columbia and Alberta, helicopters are available to ferry skiers to remote glaciers.

LEFT: Helmcken Falls, Wells Gray
Provincial Park, south central
British Columbia.

Sunset at English Bay, Vancouver.

LEFT: The Alaska Highway, south of the British Columbia-Yukon border. The highway, built by the U.S. army in seven months in 1942, winds 1,523 miles from Dawson Creek, British Columbia, to Fairbanks, Alaska.

Johnstone Strait, between Vancouver Island and the British Columbia mainland. A sailboat leaves a cove after waiting out a storm.

OVERLEAF: Mount Robson, just west of Jasper National Park, is the highest mountain in Canada at 12,972 feet.

PRECEDING PAGE: Downtown Vancouver as seen from Stanley Park, looking across Coal Harbour. During the 1920s, Vancouver's rumrunners used to moor their schooners here.

The Lions' Gate Bridge, connecting Vancouver and North Vancouver, spans the narrow entrance to Vancouver harbor.

ABOVE: North Vancouver and Burrard Inlet (Vancouver Harbor), east of the Lions' Gate Bridge. This large, exceptionally deep harbor is the busiest port on the Pacific Coast of the Americas.

BELOW: The Bloedel Conservatory, atop Little Mountain in Queen Elizabeth Park, Vancouver.

The North Pacific fishing fleet at Prince Rupert, British Columbia. Prince Rupert is also a major grain terminal.

RIGHT: Liard Hot Springs, in far northern British Columbia.

The British Columbia Parliament Buildings, right, and the Empress Hotel, left, overlook James Bay, which is part of the Inner Harbour, Victoria.

ABOVE: Sculpture in front of the British Columbia Parliament Buildings.

BELOW: Chaucer Lane, one of many attractions that gives Victoria, its olde Englishe flavor.

Part of the many miles of unbroken, unspoiled beach at Pacific Rim National Park, on the west coast of Vancouver Island.

In British Columbia you are never far from a quiet, trout-filled lake. This one is Paul Lake, near Kamloops.

St. Paul's Anglican Church, on the Gitksan Indian Reserve, Kitwanga, British Columbia. Although the church itself is only 89 years old and the bell tower just 16, the church's stained glass windows are 450 years old, a gift from St. Paul's in Bath, England.

ABOVE: A farm in the Okanagan Valley, British Columbia's rich fruit-growing region. The area's climate is designated by geographers as Mediterranean.

BELOW LEFT: The Japanese section of Butchart Gardens, 25 acres of gorgeously presented flowers and plants, near Victoria.

BELOW RIGHT: Apple harvesters in the Okanagan Valley.

35

BELOW: An Inuit family camped near Hood River, North West Territories, in the Arctic Islands. Visitors never fail to be astonished by the varied plant life that appears during the brief Arctic summer.

BELOW RIGHT: Cape Dorset, Baffin Island, North West Territories, population 725. The town is the home of the West Baffin Eskimo Co-operative, which produces the world-famous Cape Dorset Inuit soapstone carvings, prints and lithographs.

36

The Coppermine River, Northwest Territories.

The Northwest Territories and the Yukon cover an area of 1,511,979 square miles. In Dawson City, the centre of the gold rush at the turn of the century, you can visit museums, gamble at one of the few legal casinos in Canada and see an actor impersonate the poet Robert W. Service. Nahanni National Park, which is in the southwestern corner of the territories, has been included in UNESCO's list of World Heritage Sites. On the South Nahanni River, by the 300-foot Virginia Falls, you can find orchids growing. Hardy, well-heeled joggers fly up from southern Canada and the United States to compete in the grueling marathon at Arctic Bay, Baffin Island. Golfers from all over are drawn to the incomparable "browns" of the Tuktoyaktuk Golf Club. But the central fact of the north today is the struggle between the developers who are spending great amounts of money and ingenuity to extract the area's petroleum and mineral resources and the indigenous peoples—the Inuit and Dene—most of whom still follow the traditional pursuits of hunting, trapping and fishing. In many ways the northern natives are infinitely luckier than

their counterparts in the south, whose way of life was all but destroyed by white technology. The northerners have had time to prepare for the fight, and they should be able to hold their own or come to reasonable terms with the invaders. But what of the invaders? Although few southern Canadians have actually been to the north, they have always had a proprietary, affectionate regard for the region. Until recently, however, they have been mainly preoccupied with the settlement of their own regions and the east-west concerns of the nation. Only now are they turning their attention to the north in earnest; and, during the next few decades, the way that the southerners make use of those 1,511,979 square miles, will say much about the kind of country Canada wants to be.

The North

PRECEDING PAGE: Lake Laberge, Yukon, which is actually a widening of the Yukon River, north of Whitehorse, the territorial capital. Lake Laberge is where the narrator in Robert W. Service's famous poem cremated *Sam McGee*.

Two views of an Inuit summer fishing camp near Cape Dorset. The prize fish in this region is Arctic char, whose delicate flesh and flavor rival those of fresh salmon.

RIGHT: Throughout the Arctic, collections of stones like this one near Cape Dorset indicate Inuit campsites.

An aerial view of the Cape Dorset region. Part of the town can be seen at left.

ABOVE: Hikers in Kluane National Park, in the southwestern corner of the Yukon. The shiny area on the right is the Donjek glacier.

BELOW: The Champagne burial ground near Whitehorse.

43

LEFT: St. Michael's Church, Fort Rae, Northwest Territories, on the shore of Great Slave Lake. The men and women of the congregation, members of the Dogrib Indian community, sit on separate sides of the church, an old European custom introduced by early missionaries.

ABOVE: An igloo-shaped church at Frobisher Bay, Baffin Island. In 1577, to mark his safe arrival at the bay that now bears his name, Sir Martin Frobisher celebrated the first Thanksgiving on North American soil.

BELOW: Another igloo-shaped church, this one at Inuvik, Northwest Territories, near the mouth of the Mackenzie River.

45

ABOVE: An Inuit family at Grise Fiord, Ellesmere Island (population 95), Northwest Territories, Canada's northernmost community at 960 miles from the North Pole.

BELOW: Two typical stones, from which Inuit prints are made. The one on the right has been partially inked.

The winter landscape near Grise Fiord.

Inukshuks, near Pelly Bay, Northwest Territories. Inukshuks are stone cairns erected by Inuit hunting and fishing parties to tell the people who come after them where they have sighted game or fish.

Although most Arctic travel is done by snowmobile and aircraft these days, fuel in the north is very expensive and dog teams are still used for shorter journeys. Every town and village has its champion dog sled racing teams.

Think for a moment about Alberta, Saskatchewan and Manitoba, the three provinces that we loosely refer to as the Prairies. Their combined area totals 753,497 square miles. The extreme northeastern part of the region borders Hudson Bay, and from the town of Churchill, Manitoba, you can go out in small boats and play with pods of beluga whales. In the extreme southwest, in the foothills country of Alberta, you can still see cowboys riding the range, not as tourist attractions, but because that is their job. Gimli, on the western shore of Lake Winnipeg (9,465 square miles), is a resort town and the centre of the inland fishery established by Icelandic settlers. The southern half of the Alberta-British Columbia border is formed by the massive spectacle of the Rocky Mountains, and northern Alberta has one of the world's greatest oil deposits, most of it still locked in the tar sands of the Athabasca River. In Flin Flon, a mining town at about 55°N on the Alberta-Saskatchewan border, there is a 24-foot statue (designed by the American cartoonist Al Capp) of one Flintabbatey Flonatin, a character in *The Sunless City* a favorite novel of the prospectors who made the original ore strike. In Manitoba north of about 53°N, in Saskatchewan 54°N and in Alberta 57°N, agriculture gives way to a vast, almost roadless wilderness of thin forest and lakes with a largely transient population of miners, oilmen, bush pilots, trappers, prospectors, loggers and the more venturesome tourists. The official 1982/83 Manitoba road map doesn't even include the northeasternmost corner of the province. So why do we call them prairies? Only the relatively small southern portion of the Prairies is actually covered by the flat expanse of grainfields that we usually think of when we use the word "prairie."

The Prairies

LEFT: Deer grazing freely in Jasper National Park, Alberta.

The town of Banff, Alberta, is the commercial hub of Canada's oldest national park, which bears the same name. The surrounding terrain is a delight to everyone from casual hikers to the most adventurous mountaineers.

OVERLEAF: Ranchland in the Alberta foothills. On a short visit to the area in the 1930s, the Prince of Wales (later Edward VIII) was so taken by the foothills way of life that he immediately bought a ranch there.

PRECEDING PAGE: The Athabasca
River in Jasper National Park.

RIGHT: Medicine Lake, Jasper
National Park.

RIGHT: Lake Louise, Banff National Park.

BELOW: A cross-country ski marathon in Banff National Park, Alberta. The line formed by the spines of the mountains in the background is the Continental Divide, along which runs the southern section of the British Columbia-Alberta border.

OPPOSITE: A road through the often lonely vastness of the Saskatchewan prairie.

PRECEDING PAGE: A wheat field and, in the distance, grain elevators at Champion, Alberta, southeast of Calgary.

"Swathing" a grain field near Lethbridge, Alberta.

OVERLEAF: A grain stop, west of
Regina, Saskatchewan. The architect
Eric Arthur once declared, "I
believe it will take a thousand
years to develop a national style of
architecture in Canada, but I do
see a light in the west, over a grain
elevator."

63

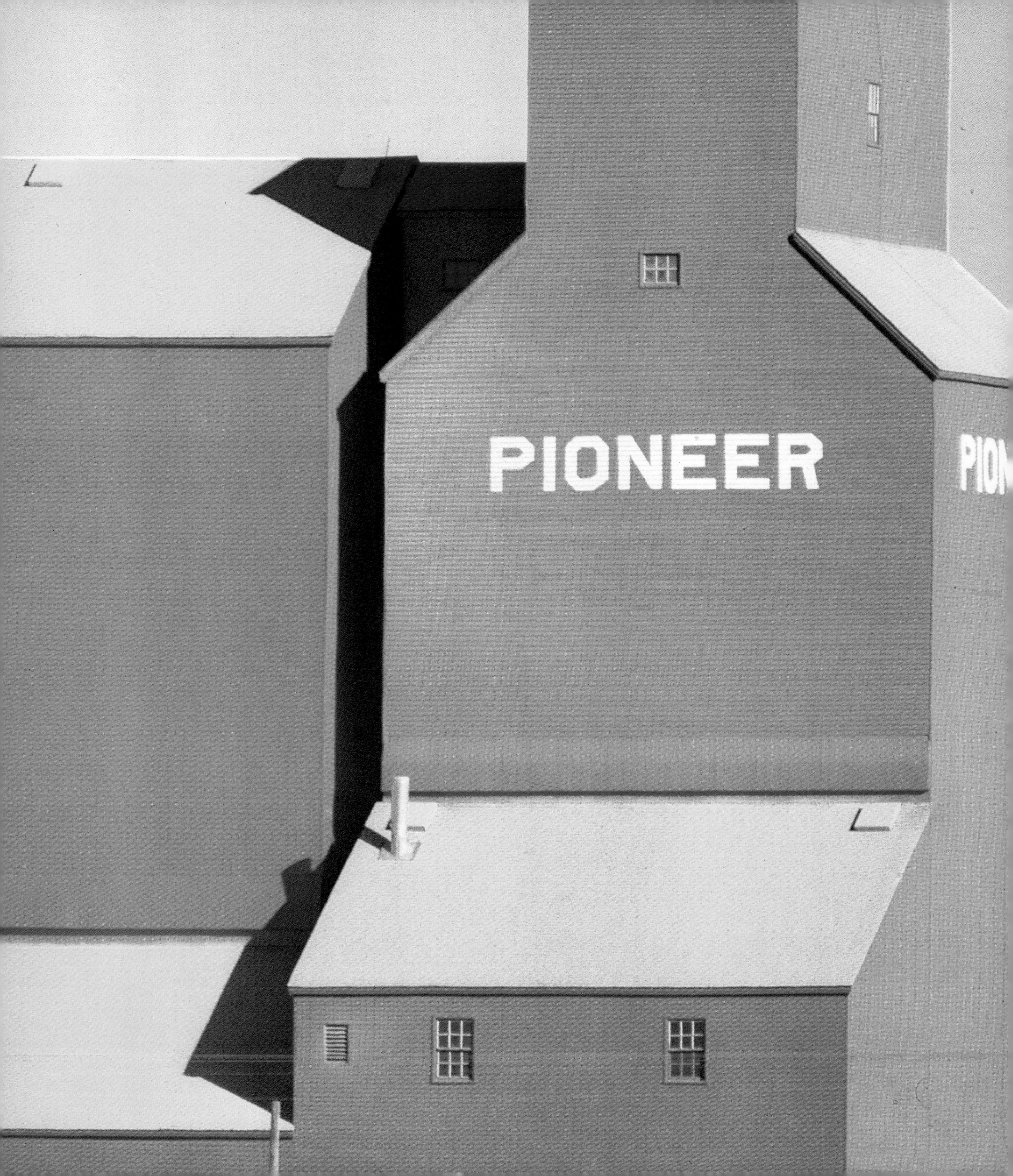
PIONEER
PION

Market gardening in southern
Saskatchewan.

ABOVE: The autumn wheat harvest
on a Hutterite farm near Lethbridge,
Alberta.

BELOW: Grain elevators near Grosse
Isle, Manitoba, northwest of
Winnipeg.

67

Abandoned farm buildings, Saskatchewan. In the drought-ridden 1930s such a sight would have meant that the residents had given up and fled the dust bowl. Today, it likely means that the people have either moved to town or to newer quarters elsewhere on their farm.

Sunflowers, their seeds ready for harvesting in Manitoba.

The Roman Catholic cemetery at Elm Creek, Manitoba, west of Winnipeg.

OVERLEAF: The famous "Leduc #1" oil well, south of Edmonton, Alberta. The development of the Leduc oil field in 1947 was the start of Alberta's postwar oil boom.

A church near Pense, Saskatchewan.

ABOVE: Downtown Calgary, Alberta. The spectacular growth of Calgary in recent years is, to most Canadians, the paramount symbol of Alberta's oil boom.

BELOW: Edmonton, the capital of Alberta, is the province's other big oil town. Booms are nothing new to Edmonton; it was the primary supply base of the 1898 Yukon gold rush.

A panoramic view of downtown Calgary.

A traditional Mormon wedding at Cardston, Alberta.

The Peace River, near the town of Peace River, Alberta. The Peace River country is Canada's last great homesteading territory, and the highway through it is the gateway to all the pioneering possibilities of northern British Columbia, the Yukon and Alaska.

ABOVE: The boisterous grandstand show at the Calgary Stampede.

Men of Vision a 12-foot statue overlooking Cochrane Ranch Provincial Historic Site. It is a memorial to Alberta's first cattlemen, and the sculptor, Malcolm MacKenzie, says descendants of the first ranchers are always saying to him, "God, that looks just like Grandad or old Uncle So-and-So."

ABOVE: Steer wrestling at the Calgary Stampede, one of the world's top rodeos.

BELOW: Alberta cowboys taking a break during the spring roundup.

RIGHT: Bronco riding at the Calgary Stampede.

Number 99, Wayne Gretzky, one of the world's greatest hockey players, is a forward for the Edmonton Oilers.

The beach at Lakeside Park, St. Catharines, Ontario, is at the north end of the Old Welland Canal, which connects Lake Ontario and Lake Erie, bypassing Niagara Falls. The beach is on Lake Ontario, and on a clear day you can see all the way across the water to Toronto.

Ontario

Ontario, Canada's second largest province (412,582 square miles), is essentially four areas: northern Ontario, southern Ontario, Toronto and Ottawa. Northern Ontario is a vast, mineral-rich portion of the Canadian Shield, extending north from Lake Huron and west to the Manitoba border. Southern Ontario, the most productive agriculture and manufacturing area in Canada, is that broad stretch of land lying between the lower Ottawa River and the tip of the peninsula near Windsor. Toronto is situated at the centre of southern Ontario, but it also has another symbolic existence in that most Canadians, with varying degrees of approval, realize that the city is the financial and communications capital of the entire country and a rival to Ottawa, the nation's political capital.

Indeed, it can be argued that Canada is a creation of southern Ontario. The fundamental fact of the Canadian identity is that we are *not* Americans, and there has never been a more resolutely un-American people than the fiercely British United Empire Loyalists who populated southern Ontario after the American Revolution and the War of 1812 (eight of the eleven National Historic Parks and Sites in the area are either fortifications or battlefields). In farming and manufacturing these people developed and prospered with a Yankee determination, and at the end of the century, when the railroads bound the nation together and made possible the great waves of immigration, southern Ontario, with its imperial dream of Canada, was in the driver's seat.

Ottawa, The Nation's Capital

LEFT: The Peace Tower and Parliament Buildings.

Dominion Day fireworks over the Parliament Buildings, as seen from the city of Hull on the Quebec side of the Ottawa River.

Skating on the Rideau Canal. On some winter days it seems the entire population of the city takes to the ice.

Changing the guard at Rideau Hall, the residence of the Governor General. The titular head of the Canadian government is Queen Elizabeth II, and the Governor General is her representative.

Toronto, The Capital of Ontario

PRECEDING PAGES: Toronto at night.

Nathan Phillips Square and the twin towers of Toronto's unique City Hall.

RIGHT: Downtown Toronto. At left is the CN Tower, the world's tallest free-standing structure (1,800 feet). The gold building is one of the two Royal Bank of Canada towers. In the foreground is the 19th-century Flatiron Building.

ABOVE: Downtown Toronto, as seen from the islands that enclose the city's harbor.

LEFT: "Little Portugal". A typical residential street in the heart of the city, where for more than a century, waves of immigrants have made their first homes in their new country.

LEFT: The main shopping arcade at the Eaton Centre. Note the realistic flock of Canada geese created by the artist Michael Snow.

No shopping area of Toronto is without at least one fresh fruit and vegetable store. This one is on Bloor Street West.

A reveler in the Caribana parade. Caribana is the annual 10-day carnival of the city's large West Indian community.

ABOVE: Winter in High Park.

BELOW: Summer in High Park.

Two views of the midway at the "Ex," the Canadian National Exhibition and Canada's largest annual fair. There are 54 permanent buildings on the grounds.

LEFT: Ontario Place, Toronto's waterfront recreation centre. Every day from late spring to early fall, thousands of visitors enjoy concerts and films and many other attractions. It is all but impossible to drag kids away from the innovative playground that they have there.

A regatta on Lake of the Woods, on the Ontario-Manitoba border.

An aerial view of Lake of the Woods.

Canoeing on Lake Kashagawigamog in Ontario's Haliburton County, about two hours north of Toronto.

A demonstration of the traditional method of making maple sugar at the Kortright Conservation Area, north of Toronto.

Farming in northern Ontario.

A lettuce crop in Holland Marsh, southwest of Lake Simcoe. The farmer is wearing special clothing to protect him from insecticides.

LEFT: Jacksons Point, Lake Simcoe, Ontario. The lake, situated north of Toronto, is the gateway to the province's cottage country.

Foxhunters near King City, Ontario. Parts of the province are even more British than Victoria, British Columbia.

OVERLEAF: Niagara Falls, Ontario, and the sightseeing boat *Maid of the Mist*.

A remote farm in the St. Lawrence Valley, Quebec. Many farms in this area have been worked by the same families for hundreds of years.

In June 1984, to commemorate the explorer Jacques Cartier's voyage to the area 450 years ago, an armada of 1,000 sailing ships from all over the world will make its way up the St. Lawrence River to the waters below Quebec City. Cartier's explorations were the basis of France's claim to the St. Lawrence Valley, and the French settled the region and held it until 1759, when General Wolfe's army sailed up the river to Quebec. But the British conquest did not mean the end of French North America. Quite the contrary. Today Montreal is the second largest French-speaking city in the world, and those charming old farms and church-steepled villages of the St. Lawrence heartland still evince the bedrock religion and the simple, rather insular values that enabled French Canada to survive, even though it was surrounded and grossly outnumbered by English-speaking Canadians and Americans. Quebec, Canada's largest province (594,860 square miles) is stronger than ever, fortified by the centuries-old struggle to remain true to its language and heritage. Recently, the Church's hold on Quebec and the province's traditional values have been challenged by a new generation of political leaders who have given the province a much more vigorous, outward-looking role in the Canadian confederation. There are even some who advocate secession from Canada. But the radical social and political transformation that Quebec is now experiencing is simply the latest and most dramatic phase of the continuing struggle to maintain the French fact in North America. As the historian Mason Wade put it in his book *The French Canadians*, "Today everything is changing, and there is general agreement that it should change. It seems clear that while French Canada is becoming more North American, it is doing so on its own terms, and that Quebec will remain French and Catholic and devoted to its traditions, in the future as in the past."

Quebec

LEFT: A lighthouse on Anticosti, the large island at the mouth of the St. Lawrence River. From 1895 to 1913, Anticosti was the private domain of Henri Menier, the French chocolate king. Now it's a provincial wildlife preserve.

The village of Ste Anne de Beaupré northeast of Quebec City, in the St. Lawrence Valley. The town is the site of a world-renowned shrine.

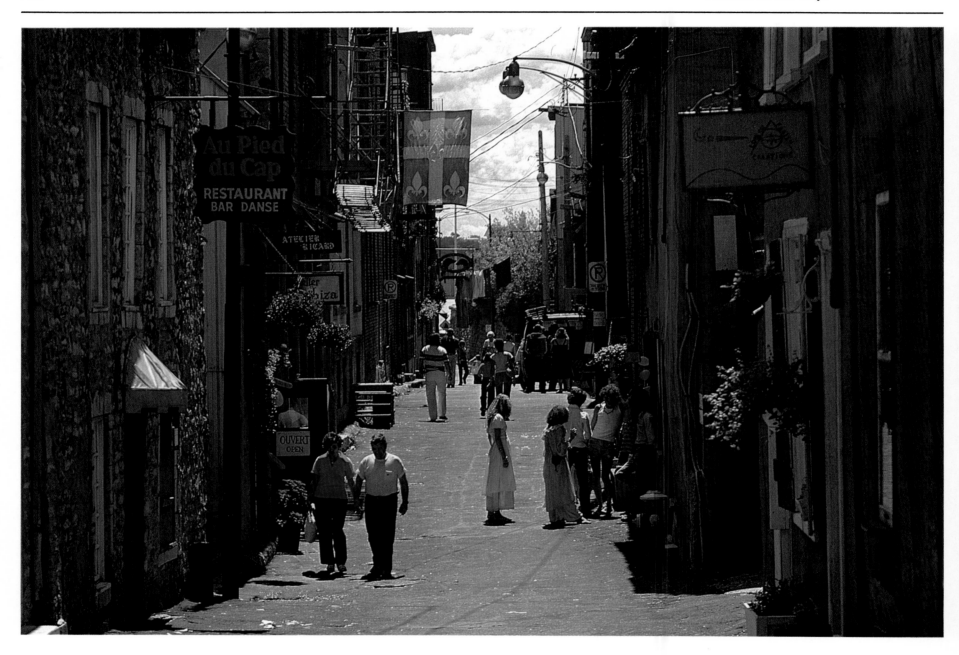

The St. Lawrence River, off the Plains of Abraham. In 1759 the British forces under Wolfe sailed to these waters, scaled this cliff and defeated Montcalm's French army outside the walls of Quebec City.

Percé Rock, in the Gulf of St. Lawrence, at the tip of the Gaspé Peninsula. The rock, 1,500 feet long and 200 feet high, is a sea bird sanctuary, protected both by legislation and natural inaccessibility.

A farm in the lovely Gatineau Hills, northwest of the Hull-Ottawa area.

Farmland on the Gaspé Peninsula.

A closer view of downtown. The city is unique in its vibrant combination of European sophistication and New York-style energy.

129

Downtown Montreal.

THE QUEEN ELIZABETH

LEFT: The midway at La Ronde, the city's big amusement park at the Man and His World exhibition centre, the site of the world's fair Expo '67.

A news vendor. If you're out on the street in the same spot, season upon season, year after year, you get to see and hear everything.

A shrine near Rivière Verte.

RIGHT: A sunset view of the St. Lawrence River, looking northwest, just east of Quebec City.

Grand Manan Island, in the Bay of
Fundy, between New Brunswick
and Nova Scotia. There are 50-
foot tides in the Bay of Fundy,
and in some spots it seems as
though the ocean disappears and
then comes back again twice a day.

Atlantic Canada

The four provinces of Atlantic Canada are Newfoundland and Labrador, Nova Scotia, New Brunswick and Prince Edward Island.

New Brunswick (27,985 square miles) is situated south of Quebec's Gaspé Peninsula and east of the State of Maine. Nova Scotia is all but an island, connected to Canada by a narrow isthmus at its border with New Brunswick; the northern part of the province, Cape Breton, is in fact an island. "The Garden Province," Prince Edward Island (2,184 square miles), lies in the bight formed by the north shores of New Brunswick and mainland Nova Scotia. Newfoundland (43,359 square miles), the easternmost part of Canada, is in the Atlantic, northeast of Cape Breton. And Labrador (112,826 square miles) is on the mainland, bordering eastern Quebec.

Canada began in the Atlantic region. Vikings are believed to have settled at L'Anse-aux-Meadows, at the northern tip of Newfoundland, about the year 1000. In 1605, at the mouth of the Annapolis Valley in Nova Scotia, Samuel de Champlain and the sieur de Monts established a settlement that grew into the colony of Acadia. And in 1864, at Charlottetown, the capital of Prince Edward Island, the Fathers of Confederation met together for the first time. The Dominion of Canada was formed three years later.

The rough beauty of Atlantic Canada has enchanted visitors for centuries, but the rugged landscape and the frequently violent ocean have not always been kind to the residents of the region. The people of Atlantic Canada live in some of the country's oldest communities, and their traditions and long history have given them a unique, forthright character that has enabled them to withstand the jagged fluctuations of the fishing, farming, lumbering, mining and shipbuilding industries. Today exploration of offshore petroleum deposits has raised expectations of an entirely new industry and an oil boom similar to the one that has recently transformed Alberta into another Texas. But the people of Atlantic Canada are not likely to become Texans. Their history and traditions will see to that.

A view from the Lookoff, Cape Blomidon, Nova Scotia. The picture shows the buildings of three farms owned by members of the Rand family. There are three more Rand farms down the road.

OVERLEAF: A farm off Highway 13, Queen's County, Prince Edward Island.

Winter farmland near Sussex, New
Brunswick.

A house in the Acadian Historical
Village, near Caraquet on the
north shore of New Brunswick.
The village is a recreated fishing
settlement reflecting Acadian life
between 1780 and 1880.

Saint John, New Brunswick,
Canada's first incorporated city,
was established by the Loyalists
who came to the area after the
American Revolution.

144

A public school and cemetery, Lunenburg, Nova Scotia. The town was founded in the mid-18th century by German settlers and became a famous shipbuilding centre.

Newtown, Bonavista Bay, Newfoundland. Newtown is a fishing village, or "outport". The church was built by the local fishermen.

A farm near Tors Cove, on
Newfoundland's Avalon Peninsula.

Wild horses on Sable Island, in the Atlantic Ocean, 177 miles southeast of Halifax. The island has always been a hazard to shipping, and the original horses are believed to have been survivors of a shipwreck.

The world's longest covered bridge (1,282 feet), at Hartland, in the Saint John River Valley, New Brunswick.

Grouchy's slipway, Pouch Cove, Newfoundland. Pouch is pronounced "pooch".

The dock at Goose Bay, Labrador. Freighters from St. John's are the primary source of supply for the lonely outports strung along the Labrador coast.

RIGHT: The Toronto-based brig *Pathfinder* off Lunenburg, Nova Scotia.

The excellent harbor at St. John's Newfoundland, was used by European fishermen long before Sir Humphrey Gilbert landed there in 1583 and claimed the area on behalf of England.

RIGHT: The navy yard at Halifax, Nova Scotia. Halifax has been an important naval base ever since the city was founded for that purpose in 1749.

Photo Credits

Mike Beedell: pages 34, 37 top, 43 top, 44

Ottmar Bierwagen: page 5

Chris Dahl: page 1

Harry Dahme: page 140

John de Visser: front cover, back cover: upper left and bottom, pages 8, 11, 14, 16, 17, 18, 19, 24, 26, 27, 28, 30, 31, 35 top and left, 36, 37 bottom, 38, 40, 41, 42, 45, 46, 47, 48, 51, 53, 58 top, 59, 60, 62, 66, 70, 71, 74, 76, 77, 78, 80 inset, 86, 89, 90, 92, 93, 94, 95, 96, 101, 103, 104, 106, 112, 115, 117, 118, 120, 121, 125, 126, 127, 128, 129, 130, 138, 142, 143, 144, 145, 147, 148, 149, 152, 154, 155

Gera Dillon: pages 122, 124, 132

Don Eldon: page 110

Ken Elliott: back cover upper right, pages 20, 29, 33, 43 bottom, 49, 52, 54, 55, 67 bottom, 73, 87, 116, 133, 134, 135, 136, 150, 153

Mike Gluss: pages 35 right, 64, 79, 82 bottom, 109

Gail Harvey: page 151

Jack Jarvie: page 67 top

George Macdonald: page 72

Robert Morton: page 21

Bob Mummery: pages 82 top, 83

E. Jane Mundy: page 131

John O'Brien: pages 12, 22, 32, 56, 88, 105, 108, 119

Courtesy of Ontario Place: page 102

Barry Ranford: page 2

John Ryckman: page 68

Carol Sherman: pages 111, 146

Alex Sokolow: page 84

Paul A. Stone: page 139

M. Sturk: page 80

Hugo Tiessen: page 58 bottom

J. Udvovskis: page 123

Ron Watts: pages 6, 97, 98, 99, 100

John Williams: page 107